# Baptism Is a Promise

written by **Katy Watkins**

illustrated by **Jeff Harvey**

**CFi**
**An imprint of Cedar Fort, Inc.**
**Springville, Utah**

ISBN 13: 978-1-4621-2184-7

Published by CFI, an imprint of Cedar Fort, Inc.
2373 W. 700 S., Springville, UT 84663
Distributed by Cedar Fort, Inc., www.cedarfort.com

Library of Congress Control Number:  2017959360

Cover design and typesetting by Jeff Harvey
Cover design © 2018 Cedar Fort, Inc.
Edited by Kaitlin Barwick

Printed in the United States of America

10 9 8 7 6 5 4 3 2 1

Printed on acid-free paper

To my parents. All of my best qualities
I stole from you. I love you.
-Katy

To Nana and Grandpa, who aren't
here anymore, but who taught me
lessons I'm still learning.
-Jeff

# DO YOU KNOW WHY YOU NEED TO BE BAPTIZED?

It is a commandment! When you keep Heavenly Father's commandments, He will bless you.

This book teaches you what baptism is and how you can follow Jesus Christ not just on Sunday, but every day!

## ON EVERY PAGE, LOOK FOR A HIDDEN PICTURE!

To reveal the picture, all you have to do is shine a flashlight behind the page or hold the page up to the light. What will you learn about baptism?

# What is baptism?

Baptism is a covenant or promise you make with Heavenly Father.

When you make and keep that promise, all of your sins and mistakes are washed away.

**Keeping covenants and promises you make with Heavenly Father is part of His plan. What covenants do you make at baptism?**

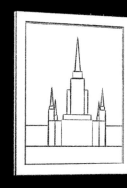

You promise to always remember Jesus Christ and to stand as a witness of Him at all times, in all things, and in all places!

# You see the new boy that just moved in being made fun of at school.
## How can you stand as a witness?

You can stick up for him and
stop the bullies!

Jesus has asked us to be kind to others.
When you are kind to others, you are
doing what Jesus would do.

You celebrate your baptism with family and friends!
It is the day that you become a member of The
Church of Jesus Christ of Latter-day Saints.
Who else is here to celebrate?

Your family members in heaven! They are happy to see you make the choice to be baptized and join the Church.

You promise to help people feel better when they're sad. One of your friends tells you that his grandma passed away. You know that he is sad, but what can you do to help?

You can listen to your friend and give him a hug!

When you help your friend, you are doing what Jesus has asked us to do.

You promise to comfort people that need it. Your friend is moving far away and she is worried about moving to a place where she doesn't know anyone. How can you comfort her?

You can comfort her by sending
her a care package!

You can still be friends from
many miles away.

You promise to be happy when other people are happy. Your teammate scores the winning goal! How can you celebrate?

You can tell them "Good job!" and give them a high five!

When you are happy for other people, you are keeping your promise to Heavenly Father.

You promise to help bear the burdens of others.
Your neighbors are sick. How can you help them?

You can take out their trash, walk their dog, or help in their yard!

When you are in the service of others, you are doing what Jesus would do.

Baptism is a promise. Heavenly Father makes a promise too when you are baptized. When you are in trouble or lost, what does He promise?

He promises that the Holy Ghost will always be there to guide and comfort you!

Like Nephi with the Liahona, He will show you the right way to go!

When you have made a mistake or done something wrong, what does He promise?

He promises that when you repent, He will forgive your sins and mistakes! Even more than that, He will remember them no more. Like Alma the Younger, you can be made clean. What a wonderful baptism gift!

# When Heavenly Father gives you a commandment what does He promise?

He promises that He will help you to fulfill it! When you keep the commandments, Heavenly Father will bless you.

Like the Stripling Warriors who went to battle and not one of them fell, Heavenly Father will give you courage and He will protect you as you serve Him.

# When you have a question, what does He promise?

He promises that when you pray in the name of Jesus Christ, the Holy Ghost will testify of the truth! Like Joseph Smith in the Sacred Grove, you can pray to know what is true.

# What else does Heavenly Father promise?

He promises that when you are worthy of the Holy Ghost, He will warn you of danger!

Like Lehi and his family escaped Jerusalem, you can escape danger before it ever comes.

Heavenly Father gave the greatest gift of all. He gave His Son so that we could return to live with Him. Jesus Christ is who you are following when you are baptized.